The Combination to God's Vault

The Combination to God's Vault

Discovering God's Will for the
Christian to Prosper Spiritually,
Physically, and Financially

Rev. Tim Oldham

Copyright © 2014 by Tim Oldham.

Library of Congress Control Number:		2014913324
ISBN:	Hardcover	978-1-4990-5902-1
	Softcover	978-1-4990-5903-8
	eBook	978-1-4990-5904-5

All rights reserved. No part of this book may be reproduced or transmitted in any form or by any means, electronic or mechanical, including photocopying, recording, or by any information storage and retrieval system, without permission in writing from the copyright owner.

This is a work of fiction. Names, characters, places and incidents either are the product of the author's imagination or are used fictitiously, and any resemblance to any actual persons, living or dead, events, or locales is entirely coincidental.

Any people depicted in stock imagery provided by Thinkstock are models, and such images are being used for illustrative purposes only. Certain stock imagery © Thinkstock.

All scripture quotations are from KJV Dake Annotated Reference Bible Version. © 1963 by Dake Publications. Trademarks are the property of their respective owners. All rights reserved.

This book was printed in the United States of America.

Rev. date: 07/31/2014

To order additional copies of this book, contact:
Xlibris LLC
1-888-795-4274
www.Xlibris.com
Orders@Xlibris.com
650062

Contents

Preface		7
Tribute		9
Chapter 1	The Vision	11
Chapter 2	Happiness of the Godly	13
Chapter 3	The Joy of Studying	16
Chapter 4	Not a Just-Enough God	19
Chapter 5	Secret of Success	21
Chapter 6	No Poor among You	23
Chapter 7	The Great Lie: Humility Means Poverty	25
Chapter 8	Our Witness	27
Chapter 9	Ask, Seek, and Knock	29
Chapter 10	Blessings Chasing	31
Chapter 11	Instant Society	34
Chapter 12	The Choice	36
Chapter 13	Don't Forget God	38
Chapter 14	Giving God His Portion	41
Chapter 15	Taking the First Step	44
Chapter 16	Good Ground	47
Chapter 17	Good Things	49
About the Author		51
About the Book		53

Preface

The teaching of the church for the last fifty years concerning the finances of the Christian has been one of contradiction to the Word of God. People have watched and followed the "big name" Christians in their fall. This is all a result of Christians not being grounded and rooted in the Word of God. They follow people, the teachings of men, and don't take time to "study to shew thyself approved unto God, a workman that needeth not to be ashamed, rightly dividing the word of truth." (2 Timothy 2:15)

As a child of God, we are to prosper in three areas, spiritually, physically, and financially. Being poor is not a sign of humbleness. It is a sign of disobedience to the Lord. We are the children of the Most High God, and we are to have all the inheritance that Jesus went to the cross to give us. This was an act of divine love, and it's time Christians stand up and claim what the enemy has stolen from God's people.

Tribute

I would like to give special thanks and tribute to a dear friend, Rev. Floyd Oldham. He has encouraged me a great deal in the Gospel of Christ. Reverend Oldham provided the original eight scriptures that this book is based on. He also greatly encouraged me to transform this study into book form. To him I give special appreciation and thanks. The original scriptures are Psalms 1:1–3, Joshua 1:7–8, Deuteronomy 28:1–14, Joshua 24:12–15, Deuteronomy 6:10–12, Malachi 3:10–11, Psalms 68:19, and Proverbs 3:9–10.

Chapter 1

The Vision

Ever since I was a little boy, I knew that I was going to be an extremely wealthy man. For me, to know that was a true revelation from the Lord because I was raised in complete poverty. Little did I know that the wealth that I was to receive was first, spiritual; second, physical; and third, financial. The best part about it is that God's riches are eternal.

As I sought the Lord more and more fervently, I learned the beauty of God's covenant promises. I learned that as a descendent of Abraham, Isaac, and Jacob, I have full rights to every covenant blessing, provided I hold up my end of the bargain. My end was to serve the Lord totally.

I remember one night God woke me up to show me a most amazing thing. It was a vision of two angels holding a silver platter with stacks and stacks of money on it. Every time I reached out and took some money from one of the stacks, more would appear in its place. Wow! Can you believe it? You can just bet I stayed up awhile mulling that one over. Later the Lord showed me the true interpretation of the vision. You see, it wasn't that the Lord was going to hand money over to me like it grew on trees. It was the same a Jacob's ladder in Genesis 28: 12–13:

"And he dreamed, and behold a ladder set up on the earth, and the top of it reached to heaven: and behold the angels of God ascending and descending on it. And, behold, the Lord stood above it, and said, I am the Lord God of Abraham thy father, and the God of Isaac: the land whereon thou liest, to thee will I give it, to thy seed."

The angels in Jacobs dream were going up and down the ladder, giving continual provision for Jacob as was promised to his father Isaac in Genesis 26:2–4:

"And the Lord appeared unto him, and said, go not down into Egypt; dwell in the land which I shall tell thee of: sojourn in this land, and I will be with thee, and will bless thee; for unto thee, and unto thy seed, I will give all these countries, and I will perform the oath which I swear unto Abraham thy father; and I will make thy seed to multiply as the stars of heaven, and will give unto thy seed all these countries; and in thy seed shall all the nations of the earth be blessed."

This same promise, God gave to Abraham in Genesis 17:6–8 and Genesis 22:15–18, which is called the Abrahamic covenant. God was visually promising Jacob that if he would continually abide in the Lord, he will prosper in all areas: spiritually, physically, and financially. The Lord showed me that he will continually provide for me in abundance as long as I serve him with all my heart, mind, and soul.

Consider the widow woman at Zarphath. She and her son were ready to die when Elijah told her to fix him something to eat.

"And Elijah said unto her, fear not: go and do as thou hast said: but make me thereof a little cake first, and bring it unto me, and after make for thee and for thy son. For thus saith the Lord God of Israel, the barrel of meal shall not waste, neither shall the cruse of oil fail, until the day that the Lord sendeth rain upon the earth." (1 Kings 17:13–14)

The flour and oil did not run out until the end of the third year of the famine. That, my Christian brothers and sisters, is just like the stacks of money on the silver platter. God never runs out. God says he will bless you in Ephesians 1:18–19:

"The eyes of your understanding being enlightened; that ye may know what is the hope of his calling, and what the riches of the glory of his inheritance in the saints. And what is the exceeding greatness of his power to us-ward who believe, according to the working of his mighty power."

God wants to show Christians his awesomeness and happiness through his mighty power.

Chapter 2

Happiness of the Godly

Psalms 1:1–3 contrasts the only two kinds of people that the Lord recognizes: the first type is the godly who are characterized by righteousness, love, and separation from the world and obedience to God. The second type of people is the ungodly who are characterized by having nothing to do with God, or represent the world and ways of ungodly counsel. Psalms 1:1–3, "blessed is the man that walketh not in the counsel of the ungodly, nor standeth in the way of sinners, nor sitteth in the seat of scornful. But his delight is in the law of the Lord; and in his law doth he meditate day and night. And he shall be like a tree planted by the rivers of water, that bringeth forth his fruit in his season; his leaf also shall not whither, and whatsoever he doeth shall prosper."

God will bless a godly man with total happiness. The Hebrew definition for blessed is happy or happiness. This is very exciting because we are called to be happy if we set ourselves apart from the world and choose to follow God totally. There is no better way to become happy than to follow God with all our heart, mind, and soul. That way, we will have a true happiness because the Lord gives it to us and it's not of our own doing. By following God, our happiness increases daily and does not stop.

We as Christians should do our very best to "walketh not in the counsel of the ungodly." Ungodly is the morally wrong or the actively bad person. It is a fine line that Christians must spend time with the ungodly to witness to them, but we do not want to have the ungodly person our primary source of fellowship. Christians must seek fellowship with other

Christians, get their counsel from a godly source, not a worldly source. We are to live in Christian virtues.

"Finally, brethren, whatsoever things are true, whatsoever things are honest, whatsoever things are just, whatsoever things are pure, whatsoever things are lovely, whatsoever things are of good report; if there be any virtue, and if there be any praise, think on these things." (Philippians 4:8)

God has all the answers if we would just seek after him and be still long enough to hear the answer. The bottom line in Philippians 4:8 is that old saying "garbage in garbage out." We cannot act like the world. In order to have God's blessing, we must be set apart from the world.

Yes, we still have to live in the world, but we do not have to act like the world. Christians need to start taking a stand to be pure and holy. No more of this wishy-washy stuff, saying I will just barely make it. Christians are to be overcomers and stay away from the world's system. In 1 John 4:4, we see we are overcomers:"Ye are of God, little children, and have overcome them; because greater is he that is in you, than he that is in the world."

We need to set ourselves apart from the world, not act better than the world but have different standards than the world. Have godly standards. Put only good things into your spirit and stay away from the sin.

I still remember the day God showed me the importance of filling my conscious and subconscious mind with things of the Lord. My girls were just babies, and they were watching a notable children's television program. The children were in the living room while my wife was in our bedroom where she couldn't normally hear the television. As she stood in front of her vanity, she began to hear in the Spirit. She could suddenly hear the words on the television that seemed so innocent and educational but in reality were very deceiving and harmful. The Spirit revealed the worldly lies being subconsciously manipulated and sown into the children. Of course, you know what happened next. Only select Christian videos were allowed in our house as well as select Christian CDs. It was time to turn off the devil vision that some people call the television set and start spending our time being influenced by godly things.

We are not even to sit in the seat of the scornful. Who are the scornful? The scornful are the mockers or the ones who make fun of someone or something.

Scornful can be described as gossip, or not telling all the truth. By picking on people, and not being godly, is sitting in the seat of the scornful. A prime example is the bars or even a social club where alcoholic beverages are served. The more a person gets intoxicated, the more they tend to talk or make fun of others, such as the boss at work, the secretary, or the girl next door. All of this type of behavior the Lord instructs us to stay away from. In order to receive God's blessings, we must be obedient. The scripture goes on to show "his delight is in the law of the Lord." (Psalms 1:2)

His delight is his pleasure or even desire in the law. It should be our desire to obey God in all things. His delight is any Christian that will serve the Lord and strive to know more about God. It is amazing how much happiness God will put in the Christian who will serve him wholeheartedly.

Chapter 3

The Joy of Studying

It is so exciting to see God's people crave to spend time with the Lord. God will give us so much happiness for serving him that others will ask, "What is it that you have to be so happy?" God has given the revelation through his Word, that it is better to serve the Lord than to serve sin. It is more fun to do godly things than anything because God's blessings are upon what you do. The more time a person spends with God, the more fun they have. The law of the Lord is his Word. In order to spend more time with God, you must study. In order to have God's blessings, you have to study. The Bible even tells us to study in 2 Timothy 2:15:

"Study to shew thyself approved unto God."

It should be our delight and our desire to study God's Word, so we as Christians can learn more about the Lord who saved us. The more we learn, the more God will pour out the blessings he has stored for us. Is that awesome or what? What can be better than learning about the Lord and being blessed while learning? We are to meditate day and night on the Lord. Meditating is to study or ponder on God's Word. We must study God's Word continuously, never ceasing. As a result, we will mature to talking to one another in psalms and hymns, quoting scripture to each other, and help each other learn about the neat things in the Word of God. This is assembling together to help, teach, and exhort one another. There is a big difference between church talk and talking about the Lord. Even the devil can church talk. Talking about the Lord and the intimate things of the Lord comes from studying.

I really enjoy having people over to my house that are willing to talk about the Word of God with me, such as studying together and having conversations about various scripture revelations. In Ephesians 3:4, the scripture tells us.

"Whereby, when ye read, ye may understand my knowledge in the mystery of Christ."

By reading and studying God's Word, we will gain knowledge and wisdom. The more we read the Word, the more we will grow spiritually in knowledge and wisdom.

The Word of God is making a comparison, showing that the student of God will grow just like a tree planted by rivers of water. The more water that goes down the river, the more water the tree roots absorb, which in turn makes the tree grow bigger and stronger. It's the same with Christians studying God's Word. The more you water your spirit, the bigger your faith and knowledge grows. A tree that has big, beautiful green leaves and strong branches produces the very best fruit. The Christian should have the same comparison—strong faith, good knowledge, and full of wisdom—from the revelations the Holy Spirit shows through studying. Rivers of water can also be described as a small channel of water like in an irrigation system.

I grew up in the southern desert of Arizona where it is dry and hot. The farmers use irrigation systems to water their fields. The water would come out of a river then go into a canal. Then water would flow into small ditches which farmers would draw water out with pipes to put water into the fields. This is how the Christian grows also. God put his Word into the spirits of men, which, in turn, wrote it out. Then we put the Word in front of us to study and grow. "He that believeth on me, as the scripture hath said, out of his belly shall flow rivers of living water." (John 7:38–39)

We can see that the streams of living water were referring to the Holy Spirit. The Holy Spirit feeds us through the Word of God. The more we are fed, the better our fruit is. With good water, and all the right nutrients, the tree will produce fruit at the right time, not falling short of perfect. The same is true with all Christians. With proper watering of God's Word and studying, we will grow and produce spiritual fruit in the right season. The tree is a parallel to the Christian life. The more it is watered, the more it grows. The more a Christian studies, the more they grow.

Years ago, I planted some fruit trees in my backyard. I was so excited about getting to have my own fruit trees. I watered them every day and put fertilizer on them once a month. The first year they grew but produced no fruit. The second year, I finally had blossoms, but they all fell off and still no fruit. The third year, I finally got some fruit.

My family and I were so excited that we all stood there and picked fruit together—all six apples and one cherry. As that season went on, my cherry tree started turning brown. I still watered it, but it kept turning more brown and pitiful-looking. Finally, I came to the conclusion that it was dead. I told my wife about the tree and that I was going to dig it up. Then came the confession. She informed me that the bugs were eating my tree. So being the loving wife she is and not wanting me to be disappointed, she put bug spray on that little tree. I must admit, there were no more bugs on that tree, so the spray did work.

The bottom line is that Christians cannot stop getting the right nutrients from God's Word in our lives. The devil is so clever at hiding the poison of sin and compromising with the world that Christians can end up just like my cherry tree—dead.

We should have a rich and fruitful Christian life. In John 15:1–8, the Word shows us that Jesus is the vine and we are the branches. If the branch does not produce fruit, it will be cut off and burned, but if the branch produces good fruit, Jesus will prune it so the branch can produce even more fruit. Without Jesus and the Word in us, we can do nothing. But with him in us, we can pattern our lives after a well-watered tree, with deep roots, that can stand any wind or rainstorm.

Chapter 4

Not a Just-Enough God

God will not bless us with more than we can deal with, so we are taught a little bit at a time. In Psalms 1:3, we can plainly see that "whatsoever he doeth shall prosper."

The Lord is showing us that whatever (which will consist of everything or all) a Christian does, will prosper. Material prosperity is God's will for those who will totally dedicate themselves to God, through studying day and night and planting themselves by the rivers of living water. Whatsoever we do or ask for, not just part, but all will prosper. My God is not a just-enough God, but an abundant God.

"I will abundantly bless her provision." (Psalms 132:15)

God will abundantly bless and provide for us. "For the Lord God is a sun and shield; the Lord will give grace and glory: no good thing will he withhold from them that walk uprightly." (Psalms 84:11)

God will not hold back his blessings from us, or his prosperity, because it is a good thing. God does not limit us to only getting our needs met, but will abundantly supply our needs and wants. The only thing that keeps us from getting our needs and wants fulfilled is complete unbelief and a lack of trust. We must trust God and believe that God can and will provide for us. We also need to trust God and say, "OK, God, you do it your way."

I cannot find anywhere in the Word of God that says God will only give us just enough. Every reference of scripture pertaining to the matter states that God will abundantly bless or more than meet your need. It is so plain that God wants to meet all your needs and wants that it is written in his Word. If God did not want to abundantly bless his followers, then Psalms 1:3 saying: "Whatsoever we doeth shall prosper" would be wrong. But Psalms 1:1–3 is portraying the image of a happy, fruitful, prosperous, strong, and well-rooted Christian that stays away from all evildoings. This Christian became this way because they committed to God through studying the Word, watering continuously, and seeking God day and night without stopping. Not when it was just convenient, but daily committed.

Chapter 5

Secret of Success

In Joshua 1:7–8 we see the benefits of being obedient:

"Only be thou strong and very courageous, that thou mayest observe to do according to all the law which Moses my servant commanded thee; turn not from it to the right hand or to the left, that thou mayest prosper whithersoever thou goest. This book of the law shall not depart out of thy mouth; but thou shalt meditate therein day and night, that thou mayest observe to do according to all that is written there in: for then thou shalt make thy way prosperous, and then thou shalt have good success."

The first part of verse 7 is telling us to be very strong and have no fear. No fear to follow God's Word and no fear of Satan. In Isaiah 43:5 it says: "Fear not: for I am with thee."

Always have courage and trust God to take care of you. Joshua was not worried or afraid when God told him to march around Jericho. He got up and told the people to start marching and was not concerned with anything else. (Joshua 6) The biggest key to success and prosperity is obedience to God. The Lord told Joshua what he had to do in order to have success, and the Lord is telling us the same thing in Joshua 1:7–8. In Acts 10:34: "God is no respecter of persons."

What God told Joshua is not just for him, but for all Christians alike. We have to be strong and courageous, not looking to the right or left no matter what the world offers. God is the direction to go. By always keeping our eyes fixed on the Lord, not circumstances or problems, we become very much more obedient to God. This way, we are not moved by the problems that come up, we are moved by the Spirit.

Wherever we go, if you take God with you, you will prosper in all things. God wants Christians to prosper abundantly with all that they do. Not just the smart financial wizards but all Christians with all that they do. There is one stipulation though; we must follow God and his Word wholeheartedly. Like Joshua was told, if he would keep God's law, then God will bless and prosper him in all that he does.

We cannot let God's law depart from us. It must be a continuous thing, to study the Word day and night in order to have complete success. By filling our hearts, minds, and mouth with the Word of God, we will be able to withstand the attacks of Satan.

I remember when a demon came to my house to visit. It was the middle of the night when I was awakened by a hard tugging on the comforter at the foot of my bed. As I sat up and opened my eyes, I saw a demon clothed in a black robe looking at me. I looked at him with no fear and said, "Oh, it's only you." Then I lay back down to go to sleep. I was very calm because I had just studied Psalms 23:4 that same evening.

"Yea, though I walk through the valley of the shadow of death, I will fear no evil; for thou art with me thy rod and thy staff they comfort me."

The Lord instantly brought that to my remembrance when the demon woke me up, so I had no fear of him. It was amazing how quickly Satan wanted to see if I would accept fear. The only thing that needs to be said now is, I thank God for teaching me when I study.

Because of that very experience, I spend more time in the Word of God, so I can be even more prepared.

We not only have to study and know the Word; we must act upon it. We can't just sit there and read the Word; we have to do what it tells us to do. You can't expect God to let you prosper and be blessed if you won't act on what God tells you to do. It just won't work that way; we have to do our part too.

We still go back to the idea of living next to the stream of living water and being planted in fertile ground. How do we know what to do? By studying the Word of God. The Lord will show you what else to do. That is how our way is prosperous and we have good success. Prosperity and good success go hand in hand. With one, you have the other. We need to be strong and courageous, not taking our eyes off of God and keeping the Word in our hearts, minds, and mouths. Not losing the Word and doing all that it tells us to do, we as Christians will have prosperity and good success.

Chapter 6

No Poor among You

I find it so exciting that God is willing to bless his children so much!

"Save when there shall be no poor among you; for the Lord shall greatly bless thee in the land which the Lord thy God giveth thee for an inheritance to possess it: Only if thou carefully hearken unto the voice of the Lord thy God, to observe to do all these commandments which I command thee this day. For the Lord thy God blesseth thee, as he promised thee: and thou shalt lend unto many nations, but thou shalt not borrow; and thou shalt reign over many nations, but they shall not reign over thee." (Deuteronomy 15:4–6)

Notice that God puts a stipulation on His blessings. That stipulation is "if." Christians must do something in order to receive God's provided blessings. We have to hearken and be obedient to the Word. Christians must obey God's Word continuously, never stopping to look to the right or to the left. Because the Lord said we will be able to lend to many and not borrow shows us that God is not a just-enough God but an overabundant-supplying God. That very scripture shows that Christians will be abundantly blessed and not just barely make it.

"Thou preparest a table before me in the presence of mine enemies: thou anointest my head with oil; my cup runneth over." (Psalms 23:5)

If your cup runs over, that means that God is going to bless you in an awesome way. Not just enough, but he will bless you abundantly. Praise God! Isn't that exciting? The key thing is total obedience to God. We must trust the Lord with our all.

One of my favorite scriptures in the Word pertaining to prosperity is 1 Samuel 2:7–8:

"The Lord maketh poor, and maketh rich: he bringeth low, and lifteth up. He raiseth up the poor out of the dust, and lifteth up the beggar from the dunghill, to set them among princes, and to make them inherit the throne of glory: for the pillars of the earth are the Lord's, and he hath set the world upon them."

God does not say he will only make the rich people wealthier. He will rise up the poor and the beggar. That was something that has always touched my heart because I knew even though I was poor, God would bless me abundantly and make me prosper.

For the Lord to make poor would be to ruin or totally destroy someone. To make rich is for God to bless the Christian with a mass of great riches. To be brought low is to be put down or humbled severely. On the other end of the table, to be lifted up is God exalting us. God does not do anything halfway; it is all or none.

These verses are to demonstrate that God owns everything. He created it so he owns it. The world, finances, all the cattle of the hills, everything is his. So God can bless us abundantly if we would only be obedient to him.

Why is it that so many Christians limit God in not believing we can be blessed and prosperous? Christians can be so blessed and prosperous that others will see it and ask, "How did you get that?" By serving the Most High God and doing what he tells me to do is how I got it.

Something I say in my home is "daddies need lots of hugs!" When I say that, no matter where my girls are, and it seems no matter how old they get, they come running to give me lots of hugs. It blesses me to see how much those two beautiful girls love me. God showed me through my girls that he is the same way with us. God wants us to be so intimate with him; we will come running to the Lord to give not hugs but quality time. By giving our quality time to God, that is giving our best and, in a sense, giving hugs. The more quality time we spend with the Lord, the closer we become and the better we know his will for our lives.

God is willing to bless and prosper the Christian for loving and spending time with him. "Beloved, I wish above all things that thou mayest prosper and be in health, even as thy soul prospereth." (3 John 2)

We know that the beloved is the Christian that serves God wholeheartedly. So we can say it is God's will for us to prosper in everything spiritually, physically, and financially. Why limit God and only prosper in one of the three? We should accept the fact that God can make it happen, and it is his will.

It is God's will for Christians to finance missions and other ministries. If we are barely making it, how can we be an asset to the spreading of the Word globally?

Chapter 7

The Great Lie: Humility Means Poverty

I find it to be so comical when I talk to people about finances. They have the attitude that in order to be humble for God you have to be poor. That is a lie from Satan himself. Satan has convinced so many of God's people that they have to be poor; they just accept it and barely make it from week to week. God does not want it to be like that. He said he would prosper us in everything.

What kind of Christian example or witness is it for the world to see us just barely getting by? Aren't we the chosen? The world sees Christians always talking about the Lord, but just barely paying their bills on time. How many people would want that kind of life? On the other hand, you have a Christian that has grabbed a good hold upon God's promises of prosperity, always talking about the Lord. That is the person who would encourage me to become a Christian and seek God more fervently.

The main purpose of writing this book is to teach God's children that it is the will of the Father to bless us, show you how to obtain his blessings, and live a pure Christian life. Then we become the ones that people want to use as an example in their lives. How can a person believe that God can save their soul, heal their body, but can't prosper them financially? It doesn't make any sense to only accept part of God's promises, when you can have it all. I personally want it all and don't want to limit him.

To get all of God's promises, we must study every day and night, communicate continuously with God, and never turn from the Word of God. Basically, serve him with all that you are.

I'm sure you've seen that bumper sticker that reads, "God said it, I believe it, and that settles it." Now the problem with that sticker is not what it says; it's that the person really has no idea what it means! I've seen it put on cars that are on their last wheel, about to fall apart, looking like it belongs in the dump. If you're going to make a statement like that, you need to know all of God's promises. You need to be an example to the readers. I don't believe we all have to drive around the most expensive car in town, but we do have to keep what we do choose to drive, in very good condition. That means keep all of the possessions God blesses us with in good condition.

Since "God said it and I believe it," now it's time to act on it. It is time to stand up and take your God given blessing. Don't just sit back and say "that settles it." All that you are doing is agreeing with God's Word. Even Satan agrees with the Word of God. Christians must act on God's Word, not just agree with it.

All of the three types of blessings . . . physical, spiritual, and financial, God wants for his children. God is not a respecter of persons, as we've learned, so he will not give a gift to one and not make it available to everyone else. Grab hold of these saints and understand God is a good God and will bless you abundantly. There is no limit. We need to understand that our spiritual lives are in direct relation with our physical lives, and all the blessings of God. The closer we get to God, the more he wants to bless us.

Put this into your heart and meditate on this: "But my God shall supply all your need according to His riches in glory by Christ Jesus." (Philippians 4:19)

This verse shows us very plainly that God will meet all of your needs, not just some or a few, but all. Again, I say do not limit God! Believe all that is written in his Word and act upon it.

Take all that God is offering, not just part. Why would you only want one dollar when the Lord is offering the bank? You only see as far as your need, but what happened to the overabundance in God's Word? It is time we stopped the little thinking and start thinking big. How can God bless you big if you only think tiny? "Both riches and honor come of thee." (1 Chronicles 29:12)

We can see that God gives riches and honor but only to those who prove to God that they want it. By studying, keeping his Word, striving to get closer to him, and trusting in him prove we want it.

Chapter 8

Our Witness

If Christians would only study for themselves, instead of just believing what the pastor or other people say, they would really know all the blessings God has for them to receive. Then we would also see some of the mighty miracles that were so evident during the time of the apostles.

"And keep the charge of the Lord thy God, to walk in his ways, to keep his statutes, and his commandments, and his judgement, and his testimonies, as is written in the Law of Moses, that thou mayest prosper in all that thou doest, and whithersoever thou turnest thyself." (1 Kings 2:3)

This verse continues to stress the fact that God will make Christians prosper only if they keep the charge of the Lord. Keep the charge means to keep the ordinance or rule of the Lord. It is pretty plain to see that God wants Christians to serve him wholeheartedly and know his Word. If we would only do what the Word says, we could prosper in awesome amounts.

We need to quit trying to do things the world's way and turn to God. We can ask ourselves, what is in it for me? Well, that is easy to answer. You will prosper in everything you do and everywhere you go. By doing things God's way, the ministry will continue throughout the world. This happens by telling others what God has done for you and by supporting God's work through your tithes and offerings. What better witness is there than by example? "And they overcame him by the blood of the lamb, and by the word of their testimony; and they loved not their lives unto the death." (Revelation 12:11)

Our testimony of what the Lord has done for us is very powerful.

Some people will listen to the words Christians say, but more people will look at your example and how you live. Christians must set a good example of what God can and will do for them. After all, isn't that the whole reason God chose a people in the first place? He chose a people to be an example for the entire world to follow. We are that people! God will always provide all that you need plus extra if you will only serve him wholeheartedly and act upon what the Word tells you to do.

I remember a time when God tested me on doing what he told me to do. I was praying and visiting with the Lord when he told me to give a young lady $184. I thought, "Lord, I will give it, but I only have $200. Are you sure you want me to do this?" The Lord told me, "Son, you still have $16 left, at least I didn't ask for it all, so give it." Then I went to her and handed her the $184. She just began to cry. After talking to her, I found out that she was praying and asking God for $184 to pay for her car insurance. It blessed me so much just to be the one used by God to bless her.

God held up his end of the promise by providing for her and also for me. It was only one week later that I received a check in the mail for $3,700—a totally unexpected surprise. I won't say this will happen to everyone or that God will immediately return the blessing. But I will say that Christians must stand up and act upon what God tells them to do without hesitation.

"Let them shout for joy, and be glad that favor my righteous cause: yea, let them say continually, let the Lord be magnified, which hath pleasure in the prosperity of his servant." (Psalms 35:27)

God actually enjoys blessing the faithful servant.

Chapter 9

Ask, Seek, and Knock

Matthew 7:7–8 are two of the most awesome and exciting verses you could imagine.

"Ask, and it shall be given you; seek, and ye shall find; knock, and it shall be opened unto you: For every one that asketh receiveth; and he that seeketh findeth; and to him that knocketh it shall be opened."

Ask means to beg, desire, require, or demand for something. We as Christians are to ask God for all that we want. We just need to make sure all of our wants line up with the Word of God. God wants his children to come to him and ask for things, just like we, as parents, want our children to ask us to give them things.

The Lord used one of our dogs to show my wife how he expects us to ask. The dog performed a simple task that a treat was normally given for. She was very busy and forgot the treat. The dog followed her around looking at her with expectance. The Lord showed us that we are to be persistent in asking what is scripturally promised, as the dog displayed persistence. Of course, the dog received her treat with contentment.

We can have all the promises of God and be blessed, but only if we ask for them. Seek them out or endeavor to get them. If you look long and hard enough, you will eventually find what you are looking for. An example pertaining to this is a job. If you go out looking for employment, maybe the first day or two you won't find one. But because God's Word says, "seek and ye shall find," you keep looking and don't quit. Then the third day, you finally get a job. Seeking is the same as chasing after God's own heart. "But seek ye first the kingdom of God, and His righteousness; and all these things shall be added unto you." (Matthew 6:33)

All the things that you want, need, and desire will be given if you will just ask God with a righteous heart. God even gives us permission to knock or beat on the door to get our prayers answered. The Lord is trying to show Christians not to quit. Knock is implying perseverance in seeking after God. Do not stop asking or reminding God for your needs, wants, and desires. By having perseverance in seeking God through studying and prayer, it helps us become more intimate with the Lord. It also shows God we are willing to do whatever it takes to have our prayers answered. Ask implies we want something or need something, while seeking implies that we have lost something or you want to find something.

When Christians pray, they must go to God with confidence and humility expecting God to hear and answer their prayer. When we seek God, seek with passion knowing God cares for you.

God gave his only son for us, so we know he cares for us and wants the very best for all of us. All those that ask God will get what they ask for. This is a promise from God not from me. You will receive and find, and the door will be opened for you.

As Christians, we need to understand, we must ask in faith not wavering even in the slightest. We can't limit God. By not having faith and putting limits on God, our prayers will not be answered. Something very interesting is the first letter of each of the three words; ask, seek, and knock spell "ask." I believe God is telling us something with this. You won't get anything if you don't ask, ask, and ask. Diligently ask until you have your prayers answered. How can God give you something if you don't tell him what you want? So start asking. It is God's Word. "If ye then, being evil, know how to give good gifts unto your children, how much more shall your Father which is in heaven give good things to them that ask him?" (Matthew 7:11)

If a worldly person can give things, then God can give awesome things. That is very exciting to know that God can give awesome things.

We as parents try to do all that we can to bless and provide for our own children. We provide them with food, clothing, protect them, and give them a home to live in. God is the same way with his children, the Christian.

God owns everything, so we know that it is possible for him to bless us in an awesome way. Is that exciting or what? God will give us good things if we ask for them. We can have perfect health, spiritual power that can't be quenched, and wealth that has no limit. Everywhere we go we can be safe. All that we do will be prosperous, and all that we put our hands to will be blessed. Why would you not want to serve the Lord with all your heart knowing this? It is so exciting to be obedient to the Lord because the blessings that go along with the obedience are unimaginable.

Chapter 10

Blessings Chasing

Deuteronomy 28:1–14 shows the Christian all the blessings that they can have if they would only hearken unto God. In the first two verses, God is telling us very plainly just to hearken unto God.

"And it shall come to pass, if thou shalt hearken diligently unto the voice of the Lord thy God, to observe and to do all his commandments which I command thee this day, that the Lord thy God will set thee on high above all nations of the earth: And all these blessings shall come on thee, and overtake thee, if thou shalt hearken unto the voice of the Lord thy God."

Hearken means to obey, so God wants us to obey him in all things. If we want God's blessings to come upon us, then we must obey God's commands and Word exactly. It is such a simple and easy request from God, but most people make it so difficult. They will do everything possible not to obey God, and then they will wonder why they have no money or are always having problems. You have to obey God to get the problems resolved.

As I've said before, all of God's blessings have a small stipulation on them; it's that small two-letter word called "if." If you do this, then I will do that. This is what God is telling Christians. We must act on what God says, serve God with a whole humble heart to get all of his awesome blessings.

One part of Deuteronomy 28:2 that I really like is where it says "these blessings will overtake thee." We won't have to go looking for blessings; they will find us and overtake us. Overtake you means they will catch up to you and pass you. All of God's blessings will catch up to the diligent

Christian. God's blessings will even chase you down the street. Could you imagine a blessing chasing you down the street?

I remember when an officer of the law pulled me over while I was going home one day. As I was stopping, I was thinking "what did I do wrong?" When he walked up to my car, I recognized who he was. He was a Christian brother I knew. He told me that he recognized my car and stopped me just to talk. What a blessing that was to get no ticket! Actually, I had witnessed to this officer several weeks before, and he had accepted the Lord. He wanted to tell me he was still reading God's Word.

This may be an extreme case of a blessing chasing you down the street, but for him to be so proud to stop me and tell me that he was still in God's Word was a major blessing to me. Often when someone comes to know the Lord, that's where they stop. They don't start to study for themselves. Anyway, the officer and I stood there on the side of the road just praising God.

Another example of a blessing chasing me down the street was with a piece of land. I had decided to sell a portion. With no advertisement or realtor, a man came out to where I was cutting wood and offered me over three times what I had paid for it only a year before. I had prayed, "Lord, I want to sell a portion of this land, please bring a buyer and I want no less than three times what I paid for it." Only God could cause such a meeting and a desire for that land. God's Word is true!

The first fourteen verses of Deuteronomy 28 tell of all the blessings that we as Christians can have if we hearken to the voice of God. Those blessings are:

1. We as Christians will be set on high and blessings will overtake us v. 1
2. Be blessed in the city v. 3
3. Blessed shalt thou be in the field v. 3
4. Blessed shall be the fruit of thy body (our children) v. 4
5. Fruit of thy ground (all our crops or gardens) v. 4
6. Fruit of thy cattle (ranches with numerous livestock) v. 4
7. Increase of the kine (cows or oxen) and the flocks of thy sheep v. 4
8. Blessed shall be thy basket and thy store (storehouses full of supplies) v. 5
9. Blessed coming and blessed going v. 6
10. The Lord will cause thine enemies to be smitten (victory over all enemies) v. 7
11. The Lord will command our land to be productive and all that you put your hand to v. 8

12. The Lord shall establish thee as holy people v. 9
13. All people shall see us as a witness and example v. 10
14. People will be afraid of thee v. 10
15. The Lord shall make thee plenteous in goods v. 11
16. The Lord shall open unto thee his good treasure v. 12
17. Heaven to give rain unto thy land v. 12
18. Bless all the work of thine hand v. 12 (bless all that you do)
19. Thou shalt lend unto many nations and thou shalt not borrow v. 12
20. The Lord shall make thee the head, and not the tail v. 13
21. Thou shalt be above and not beneath v. 13

All of these blessings can be yours only if you will hearken or do the commandments of the Lord. If I had not been obedient in giving the young lady the $184, there is no telling what may have happened.

We need to start thinking on what God can and will do for us, rather than thinking on what can't be done. Remember that nothing shall be impossible with God. We just need to accept that as a fact and go forth. If God can part the sea, raise the dead, heal the sick, blind and lame, why do so many Christians have such a difficult time believing God can and will meet all their needs? The scriptures so far have shown very plainly, that it is God's will for all of our needs to be met. Not just barely, but more than abundantly.

Something all Christians must understand and accept is the fact that God gave us all a choice. Choose right or wrong, salvation or hell, sin free or sin, obedience or disobedience. God's blessings are still conditional based on whether we are obedient or not.

An interesting point to make is all the blessings listed in Deuteronomy 28: 1–14 cover every area of a person's life. Not just part, but every area possible. God loves his children so much He's covered every area to make sure we will be blessed. Some say God does not want us to have much money, but look at Deuteronomy 28:11: "And the Lord shall make thee plenteous in goods . . ."

Plenteous in goods is abundant prosperity. God will bless you with more than enough finances or money to meet your needs. There is no better feeling than being able to wake up in the morning knowing you serve the most high and mighty God that meets all your needs. God wants us to be in the position of having all our bills paid on time, food in the house, and able to further the ministry. That is the best way to witness to our neighbors and friends through our example of being good stewards with what God gave us.

Chapter 11

Instant Society

God is so willing to bless his children that he will even drive out all the evil people from the land they occupy, so his chosen people can have the land already prepared for them.

"And I sent the hornet before you, which drove them out from before you, even the two kings of the Amorites: but not with thy sword, nor with thy bow. And I have given you a land for which ye did not labor, and cities which ye built not, and ye dwell in them: of the vineyards and olive yards which ye planted not do ye eat. Now therefore fear the Lord, and serve him in sincerity and in truth; and put away the gods which your fathers served on the other side of the flood, and in Egypt; and serve ye the Lord. And if it seems evil unto you to serve the Lord, choose you this day whom ye will serve; whether the gods which your fathers served that were on the other side of the flood, or the gods of the Amorites, in whose land ye dwell: but as for me and my house, we will serve the Lord." (Joshua 24:12–15)

God drove out the people using hornets, not a sword or a bow, so the tribes of Israel could just walk in and settle down not having to fight. God wanted to bless his children so much that he gave them land that already had homes built and gardens planted so that they wouldn't have to labor for it.

I suppose you could call this an instant home and farm. Just like what we have now in an instant society. People think we came up with the idea of instant everything like coffee, food, microwave dinners, etc. It looks like God already had the idea set up. He told the tribes of Israel to just move on into the city, the food is growing, homes are built, and everything is in place. Are you beginning to see and understand how much God wants to bless his children?

By accepting Jesus Christ as your Lord and savior will make you a part of God's children. Joshua 24:14 stays in line with all of the other references about God blessing his people: "Now therefore fear the Lord, and serve him in sincerity and in truth."

To serve him means to worship him without question or doubt. To serve God in sincerity is without blemish or without spot. Christians are to worship him totally committed without wavering or looking to the right or left. We are to keep our eyes focused totally on the Lord. As soon as we take our eyes off of the Lord, we will start to fall just like Peter began to sink in the sea. (Matthew 14:30)

It is so exciting to submit to God totally without wavering because God was so willing to bless the Israelites. Since God is not a respecter of persons, that means he will have the same willingness to bless you and I. Can there be anything better than to have all of God's blessings? God will give you land and possessions that you did not work for just because you serve the Lord with all your heart and all your might, diligently seeking after him.

One thing that needs to be pointed out is in Joshua 24:14: "Put away the gods which your fathers served on the other side of the flood, and in Egypt; and serve ye the Lord."

What this part of the verse is talking about is idol gods or evil doings. God will not tolerate worshipping idols and serving sin. Many people don't realize that the god or idol of the world today is money. I have seen so many people fall because of their love of money.

You will not be blessed with abundance until you put away the false gods that control you. Stop worshiping the money and worship the Lord who can give you the abundance. Remember, Exodus 20:5 tells us that God is a jealous God and will not stand for his children to bow down to something or someone other than him.

Chapter 12

The Choice

God has given every person alive the right to choose. Choose right or wrong, sin or sin-free. God will not go against our own will; he will just urge and nudge us to make the right choice. God wants us to pick him and not look back. By looking back, we take our eyes off the Lord and fall. "Choose you this day whom ye will serve . . ." (Joshua 24:15)

God guarantees everyone at least one chance to choose him. After that, the ice gets thinner every day. You don't know if you will have another chance to choose him or not. As far as I am concerned, why take a chance with this one?

I remember a pastor once preached a sermon on salvation that really caught my attention. He said, "If you choose God and live a humble life, helping others, doing good and serving the Lord . . . if when you die, you find out there really was no God, you didn't lose anything. You just lived a good life." Then he added, "If you lived for the world, doing evil and had no kindness in you, then died and found out that God was real; then you went to hell because you didn't accept the Lord."

It made me so sad to hear a pastor use that type of example because it was obvious he didn't have a real revelation of the Lord. You can choose God and receive all the blessings he has to offer, or you can choose not to serve God and receive all the curses that are mentioned in Deuteronomy 28:15–68.

Just living a good life is an embarrassment to Christianity. We are his chosen! Quit making God look weak in the eyes of the heathen! If a person were to sit down and count all the curses in these verses, they would find 124 curses. In the first fourteen verses of Chapter 28, there are only twenty-one blessings. The amount of curses alone can give a person the understanding that God doesn't take too kindly to the idea of not being an able example.

Joshua 24:15 finishes up by saying, "As for me and my house, we will serve the Lord."

When you first become a Christian and take the stand of "no more compromise," you take a lot of ridicule and are made fun of. But in the end, when God says, "Well done, thy good and faithful servant," it's all worth it.

Once a Christian grasps the concept of all the blessings that God has set aside for those who will seek him diligently, and understands what God will do for them, there is absolutely no limit to what you will do or can have.

Remember that Matthew 7:11 tells us God can give much better things than the people of the world can give. Christians need to keep their eyes on the Lord, and expect God to bless them.

It is time to quit playing church and playing the games with the devil. Get our eyes off the big preachers and other famous people, and put our eyes on God without wavering. Those people that some Christians have been watching don't help with your needs or pay your bills. Only God can do that. If we try to take God's job and give it to people, that is the same as serving an idol.

Chapter 13

Don't Forget God

God will not take second place to anyone. Any type of insincerity or fallacy is an abomination to God, and he will not accept that type of worship. Remember 1 Chronicles 28:9: "For the Lord searcheth all hearts, and understandeth all the imaginations of the thoughts . . ."

We can't hide any impure motives and thoughts from the Lord. God wants to be served wholeheartedly. Now the only question is are you willing to give your all to God?

Deuteronomy 6:10–12 goes into even more detail about God giving Christians something they didn't work for:

"And it shall be, when the Lord thy God shall have brought thee into the land which he sware unto thy fathers, to Abraham, to Isaac, and to Jacob, to give thee great and goodly cities, which thou buildest not, and houses full of all good things, which thou fillest not, and wells digged which thou diggest not, vineyards and olive trees, which thou plantedest not; when thou shalt have eaten and be full; then beware lest thou forget the Lord, which brought thee fourth out of the land of Egypt, from the house of bondage."

God is making it very plain that he will give us things that we have not worked for, or done anything to deserve the blessings, other than serve him with all our hearts. It must be God's will to bless and prosper those Christians that are willing to give their all to the Lord, because of all the extremes that God is going to, to prove this to us. Since God is so willing to bless those that are sold out for God, it would be downright silly not to trust completely in him.

Remember, we must never forget that it is the Lord that gives us the abundance, it is not of ourselves. When we forget where all the blessings came from, they will all be taken from us, and then we will be destroyed. All too often, Christians that have been blessed abundantly have forgotten God because they are thinking all their needs are met and their bills are paid. They say, "I did this or I did that, it was all the right choices I made." All during this time this person is not recognizing the fact that God is the one that made the choices and direction right. When a Christian gets like this, it is called foolish pride. Proverbs 16:18 gives us a little explanation about pride: "Pride goeth before destruction, and an haughty spirit before a fall."

Forgetting God can be extremely dangerous in many ways. When forgetting takes place, some Christians stop paying their tithes, withhold from God, and then start to depend upon themselves instead of God. I have watched Christians that were so wealthy they could have anything they wanted, forget God. God gave all their wealth to them and when they forgot about God and only thought of themselves, God took their blessings.

In one case, this man had a very thriving construction business. He was doing extremely well with building custom homes in the very rich side of town. He became full of pride and very arrogant. He didn't want to have anything to do with the regular middle class person. He stopped paying his tithes and finally quit seeking God altogether. I repeatedly warned him not to play this game with the Lord. After one month, the stock market crashed and the building business took a nosedive. He lost everything and became very bitter toward God.

"But thou shalt remember the Lord thy God: for it is he that giveth thee power to get wealth, that he may establish his covenant which he sware unto thy fathers, as it is this day." (Deuteronomy 8:18)

We can see from this verse that it is God that gives power to become wealthy and prosperous. Misuse of God's blessings and pride can result in God taking them away from you.

As sad as it is to say, most Christians are still living with just barely enough because they don't look to God as their source. They will look to themselves, their paychecks or their employers. In order to have what God wants us to have, we must start looking to God.

All through history, man-made ways have failed, but God has never failed. God is the only source that Christians need because he does not run out or end. He owns it all, not just part, but all. "The silver is mine, and the gold is mine, saith the Lord of host." (Haggai 2:8)

God comes right out and says two of the most precious metals are his. The exciting part is that he wants to share it with the dedicated Christian.

God is our source and will supply all of our needs, so long as we don't forget him. Once we forget him just like this other individual did (the man with the thriving construction business), the Holy Spirit will pull away from us along with God's blessings.

We can't put our trust in the world system or ourselves; we have to trust God only. By remembering who our source is, will keep the blessings and prosperity flowing in our direction. These blessings won't stop or dwindle away. Christians will have the abundance to not only meet their daily needs, but enough to further the ministry as well.

The two major reasons why God wants us to be so prosperous are to further the work of God through giving and helping others, and to show the world who is serving the true God.

Chapter 14

Giving God His Portion

Something that must not be forgotten is the tithe. Some Christians think that tithing is not important, but God says otherwise. In Malachi 3:10–11, God is very plain with his command and challenge:

"Bring ye all the tithes into the storehouse, that there may be meat in mine house, and prove me now herewith, saith the Lord of hosts, if I will not open you the windows of heaven, and pour you out a blessing, that there shall not be room enough to receive it. And I will rebuke the devourer for your sakes, and he shall not destroy the fruits of your ground: neither shall your vine cast her fruit before the time in the field, saith the Lord of hosts."

The Lord will bless a Christian in an awesome way, but God expects to get a portion of the blessing to further the work of the ministry.

God issues a challenge to every Christian with these two verses in Malachi. The Hebrew definition for tithes is a tenth or tenth part. In Malachi 3:10, the Lord is telling us to give back, a tenth or 10 percent to him.

Some say you have to give the tenth to your local body, others say you can give it to a ministry of afar. I say put it where God tells you to—just as long as you give back to God his tenth willingly with no strings attached. That is the way we need to start looking at our income: this is God's part (the 10 percent), and this is my part (the 90 percent). God is not asking for much with just 10 percent. What would happen if God wanted the 90 percent instead? It would be a mad panic.

We need to learn to live on only 80 percent of our income instead of the 100 percent. By living on 80 percent, you will have the tenth part for God and the other tenth part to pay yourself. If you can learn to pay yourself a tenth also, then you could accumulate a very nice savings in a short period of time. By doing this, you will always have money when you want something extra or if something unexpected comes up.

I learned this lesson when I was very young just by watching my family. The very minute they got money in their hands, they would spend it all and have nothing left for a time of need.

God's purpose for the tithe was twofold. One reason was to support the ministry work, and the other was to set in motion the covenant blessings of God for his children. God set it up so the Israelites were required to give 10 percent of their livestock and crops. This was because God wanted them to recognize the fact that it was him that blessed them with what they had not what they had done themselves. It is the same today; we need to recognize the fact that God abundantly blesses us with what we have. Giving the 10 percent back to God sets into motion the awesomeness of God's abundant provision.

Some Christians think that they can't afford to tithe or even think, "Why should I tithe, I have all that I have because of me anyway?" First, Christians can't afford not to tithe. If you don't, you are not being obedient to God's Word. Second, that is the exact way of thinking Satan wants us to have. Satan's purpose is to bind and destroy you as well as destroy your financial blessings by keeping you in poverty and just barely getting through life. By getting the Christian to withhold from God and not tithe, this stops the flow of God's blessings. Once God's blessings stop, the Christian will go down fast like a sinking ship.

When the blessings and abundant provisions stop the bondage and financial despair starts. The only way to keep God's blessings coming and getting out of the financial despair is by tithing back to God and being obedient in all areas of Christian life.

You don't tithe with want you can afford, but with what you have, just as the Israelites did. Through giving of you tithes, God intended that there be no lack in the house of the Lord. (Malachi 3:10: "That there may be meat in mine house . . .")

There are very few places in the Bible where God tells us to test him. "And prove me now herewith, saith the Lord of hosts . . ." (Malachi 3:10)

God is telling us to prove him. Prove in Hebrew is *baachan*—to test, to examine, to try. Prove in Greek is *dokimazo*—to test with the expectation of approving. This verse is totally mind- boggling when you stop and think about it in the natural realm. God is telling us to prove or test him. Try and see if you can out-give God with your tithes.

The one thing that we need to remember is God owns everything.

How could a person in their right mind think they could out-give the God who owns it all? There is just no way possible, especially since our God is willing to over abundantly bless his obedient children.

God's storehouse is full, and all the blessings that he has are just sitting there waiting for the obedient Christian to set into motion God's promises of providing for them.

Think of Joseph in Genesis 41. The Lord showed him to gather up food from around the land to fill a storehouse. When the famine came, the inhabitants of the land could buy food from him to survive. Through Joseph, the whole land was blessed and provided for. In the same way, God's storehouse is continually full. We are to be a blessing to others in time of need and finance the furthering of the kingdom of God.

Chapter 15

Taking the First Step

Throughout the Word of God, he wants the believer to take the first step, for example Matthew 7:7–8: "Ask and it shall be given for every one that asketh receiveth."

You have to ask first. Another example is in Matthew 12:13: "Stretch forth thine hand. And he stretched it forth; and it was restored whole, like as the other."

The Lord told this man to do something first, and if he was obedient, then he would be healed. "Stretch forth thy hand." You put your hand out here even if you can't stretch it out. As the man stretched his arm out to Christ, the healing process began to take place.

As you can now see, God wants us to take the first step. "Try me and prove me" is what God is telling his people. God is telling Christians so plainly it is time to take the first step to see what will happen. We need to stand up and heed to the Holy Spirit by taking this first step before it is too late.

Now we need to act and find the ministry that God wants you to help, whether it be your home church or another ministry that is true to God's Word. God's Word is the ultimate force, but without believers acting upon it, they will live a defeated life. You have to start first, and then God will do his part, and all your needs will be met.

To continue on, in Malachi 3:10, it says, "If I will not open you the windows of heaven, and pour you out a blessing, that there shall not be room enough to receive it."

This proves that God will abundantly bless you. That is just one of the many awesome promises God has made: to pour out more that we can contain.

I find it so sad when I talk to other Christians that are struggling so much and just getting by. They have put God in a bottle with a tight lid and won't accept the fact that he can and will bless them financially. First, they won't tithe, and then they won't believe that God will meet their needs.

Some limit God by saying, "God will only help them with the big things." That is how the devil has so many believers in bondage. The obedient Christian that is willing to give all to the Lord will have the blessings running over to share with others. God will give so much that it will be overflowing. "Give, and it shall be given unto you, good measure, pressed down, and shaken together, and running over." (Luke 6:38)

There it is again, the believer acting first and then God meeting the need more than abundantly. After your first step, God will meet you. Even salvation is a situation of us acting first, and then Jesus came into our lives to fill us with God's love and salvation.

Many Christians are afraid to ask God for financial blessings, but it is OK to do so. It's a good thing to give to God expecting to receive a blessing. God wants his children to give in worship and from a pure heart. This shows God that we are glad for what he has done with and for us.

God has promised to open the windows of heaven and pour out the blessings on us. This is the same as reach forth your hand and be healed; you have to start tithing first. In 2 Corinthians 9:6, God gives us an interesting perspective: "But this I say, he which soweth sparingly shall reap also sparingly; and he which soweth bountifully shall reap also bountifully."

He loves a cheerful giver, not just in tithes but in all things. Give your best to others, and God will give his best to you. We have the choice to give unto God either sparingly or bountifully. God will bless you according to how you give. It is not how much you have to give, it's your heart in giving. Believers need to stop and do a heart check when they are tithing and giving. Are you giving out of thankfulness for what God has given to you? Remember that God owns it all.

A good example the Word of God gives is in Luke 21:1–4, which is referring to the poor widow woman casting in her two mites. She gave all that she had expecting God to meet her needs and abundantly bless her. God considered what she gave to be very much because she gave from her heart all that she had and with total dedication to him.

Now my purpose is not to tell you to go out and give all you have to the church but be willing to give as God urges you to, no matter whom it is he says to give to. Do what he tells you to do without question then expect to be blessed.

"Rebuke the devourer for our sakes." (Malachi 3:11)

The Lord is going to place a protective hedge around his faithful children to protect them and make sure their needs are all met. God will protect all that we have and all that we are.

Another example that shows God will protect and bless his children is in Exodus 23:25–26:

"And ye shall serve the Lord your God, and he shall bless thy bread, and thy water; and; I will take sickness away from the midst of thee. There shall nothing cast their young, nor be barren, in thy land: the number of thy days I will fulfill."

God tells us that for those who serve him, they will be blessed and all their needs taken care of. That is just so awesome to have all your worries and needs taken care of by the Lord. Christians should not have barren land or unprofitable crops. God is so willing to meet our needs that he tells us over and over in his Word. We just have to be obedient to all his commands. As funny as it sounds, the more you give, the more you get as long as you give with an "I love you, Jesus" heart.

Chapter 16

Good Ground

In Proverbs 3:9–10, we find two commands and two blessings that go right along with God's abundant provision: "Honor the Lord with thy substance, and with the first fruits of all thine increase: so shall thy barns be filled with plenty, and thy presses shall burst out with new wine."

Substance means wealth or riches. So honor God with all your riches and wealth. We should be happy and excited to tithe unto God with all that we have. The first fruits are the first part of all that we have been given.

Why put $100 into the world's system when your odds of reaping a return are extremely slim, or you have to wait ten years or more for it to "mature?" If you sow that same $100 into a ministry that God has led you to invest in, you are guaranteed to reap a reward. In Matthew 13:8, scripture shows us that we can even reap a hundredfold: "But other fell into good ground, and brought forth fruit, some an hundred fold, some sixty, some thirty fold."

I once knew a pastor that actually played the lottery with his church's money. Can you imagine such a thing to do with God's money? Instead of using the money to prayerfully sow into another ministry to further expand the Word of God, (which is a sure investment) he gambled it in the world's system and thought God would allow him to "get rich quick." Even if it was extra money, it still should have been sown into a ministry. Think of all the money wasted that this pastor could have been reaping a harvest on? It is so sad to hand God's abundance over to the world. That is not a good steward.

God will not hand his children the overabundance until he has taught them how to "walk in the blessings." One day, I read in the newspaper that 90 percent of the people that had won the lottery were broke and had nothing to show for their wealth within three years. But you say, "I am different, I'll invest." Get real! You have to be taught by God how to walk in the blessings. God, in his awesome and infinite wisdom, will teach his children every single step of the way to be able to handle the blessings. As your finances grow, wisdom must also grow. God will never lead you out on a limb and drop you off or leave you hanging. "For he hath said, I will never leave thee, nor forsake thee." (Hebrews 13:5)

God will always finish the good work he has started. "For he will finish the work . . ." (Romans 9:28)

God is the only investment and investments broker that a Christian needs. In Matthew 19:26, it says, "But with God all things are possible."

We see God can do all, so why not tithe into something God sanctions? Jesus even taught on tithing throughout the New Testament. In Matthew 23:23, we see Jesus telling the scribes, Pharisees, and hypocrites that it is a good thing to tithe. If Jesus is saying it is a good thing, then we as believers better be tithing and giving.

Paul taught in 1 Corinthians 16:2, "Upon the first day of the week let every one of you lay by him in store, as God hath prospered him, that there be no gatherings when I come."

The more a Christian tithes, the more God will prosper them, and then the more they can tithe. It becomes a snowball effect. Tithing is proof of your obedience and gratefulness for all of the blessings God has given to you. In 2 Chronicles 31:4–21, we see the children of Israel tithing and reaping abundantly because they were faithful to God. Material and spiritual blessings are certainly tied directly to the simple fact of obedience and tithing.

Chapter 17

Good Things

God will give good things to his children every single day. In Psalms 68:19, the Word tells us so: "Blessed be the Lord, who daily loaded us with benefits, even the God of our salvation. Selah."

Benefits are defined as any good thing. It is very exciting to know God will daily provide for the believer as well as support us. There are many areas in which God will support us. He will keep us safe and make sure we are protected. Some people will laugh and say it was just luck that you were protected or you are lucky for what you have, but I believe it's God. I can't find any word in the Bible that resembles the word luck. I find blessing, protection, covenant, and guidance from the Lord, but no luck.

I remember one time God protected me while I was driving home. I was playing a praise and worship tape, worshiping the Lord and talking to God. I came around a blind corner to find a very large truck pulling a big boat trying to pass another car in a no passing zone on my side of the road. I didn't have any time to react, pull over, or stop. I just said, "Oh God." With canyons on both sides and no margin, I had nowhere to go but head on into the truck. Needless to say, God supernaturally set me over the truck and trailer as if it weren't even there. After that, I stopped to thank God for his protection and to regain my composure. The other car being passed stopped too. I am thankful for the whole situation because it became a great opportunity to witness to him.

There is no end to what God will do to protect those who will give their all to him. In Daniel 3, God's Word shows us the extreme of his protection for his servants. It's the familiar story of Shadrach, Meshach, and Abednego. God protected them in such a way that it would prove to the world who served the real God. God is still doing the same thing today. He wants to prove to the world who the true God is through his children. "For the Lord God is a sun and shield: the Lord will give grace and glory: no good thing will he withhold from them that walk uprightly." (Psalms 84:11)

As the sun gives heat, illuminates, and sustains life on the earth, so the Lord God will protect, defend and bless those who faithfully serve him. The Lord promises to be the supplier of all good things. "The young lions do lack, and suffer hunger: but they that seek the Lord shall not want any good thing." (Psalms 34:10)

The only excuse for the faithful Christian to be in want is unbelief and ignorance of truth. We must believe and accept the Word as truth, and not pick and choose the scriptures we want to believe in order to continue in compromise and slothfulness. It's time to stand up and be the child of God you have been called to be.

About the Author

Rev. Tim is an ordained minister of the Gospel with the God-given title of a prophet. He lives a life of no compromise with the Word of God. Reverend Oldham travels to minister where called of God, manifesting the gifts of the Spirit as required by all true servants of Jesus Christ.

"And these signs shall follow them that believe; in my name shall they cast out devils; they shall speak with new tongues: they shall take up serpents; and if they drink any deadly thing, it shall not hurt them; they shall lay hands on the sick, and they shall recover." (Mark 16:17–18)

His desire is to win souls for Christ and to encourage Christians to seek a deeper revelation and relationship with the Lord and to prove to the world that Jesus Christ is the real and true God.

IS A DEEPER REVELATION OF GOD WHAT YOU'RE LOOKING FOR?

Rev. Tim presents *THE COMBINATION TO GOD'S VAULT* as a tool to teach Christians how to obtain the covenant blessings promised to every believer. Along with Rev. Tim's firm belief of no compromise and holiness, he has the God-given gift to teach people how to become disciples, not just converts.

"God's gifts are not to be flaunted. The people are to be taught that 'God is no respecter of persons.' What we have, you can have too. My purpose is to teach you how to get it. All God needs is a willing vessel."

It is with this belief that Rev. Tim shares the revelations of the Lord, to inspire and encourage you in your walk with Jesus Christ.

Rev. Tim's teachings are strong and firm for the Christian who wants more!

About the Book

The teaching of the church for the last fifty years concerning the finances of the Christian has been one of contradiction to the Word of God. People have watched and followed the "big name" Christians in their fall. This is all a result of Christians not being grounded and rooted in the Word of God. They follow people, the teachings of men and don't take time to "study to shew thyself approved unto God, a workman that needeth not to be ashamed, rightly dividing the word of truth." (2 Timothy 2:15)

As a child of God, we are to prosper in three areas, spiritually, physically, and financially. Being poor is not a sign of humbleness. It is a sign of disobedience to the Lord. We are the children of the Most High God, and we are to have all the inheritance that Jesus went to the cross to give us. This was an act of divine love and it's time Christians stand up and claim what the enemy has stolen from God's people.

Made in the USA
Las Vegas, NV
24 February 2021